KEEPING HEALTHY

Personal Hygiene

Text by Carol Ballard
Photography by Robert Pickett

HODDER
Wayland

an imprint of Hodder Children's Books

TITLES IN THE KEEPING HEALTHY SERIES:

• Personal Hygiene • Eating • Safety
• Exercise • Relationships • Harmful Substances

© 2004 White-Thomson Publishing Ltd

Produced by White-Thomson Publishing Ltd
2/3 St Andrew's Place, Lewes, BN7 1UP

Editor:	Elaine Fuoco-Lang
Consultant:	Chris Sculthorpe, East Sussex, Brighton & Hove Healthy School Scheme Co-ordinator
Inside design:	Joelle Wheelwright
Cover design:	Hodder Wayland
Photographs:	Robert Pickett
Proofreader:	Alison Cooper
Artwork:	Peter Bull

Published in Great Britain in 2004 by Hodder
Wayland, an imprint of Hodder Children's Books.
Hodder Children's Books, a division of
Hodder Headline Limited, 338 Euston Road,
London, NW1 3BH.

British Library Cataloguing in Publication Data
Ballard, Carol
    Personal Hygiene. - (Keeping Healthy)
    1. Hygiene - Juvenile literature 2. Health -
    Juvenile literature
    I. Title
    613

ISBN 0 7502 4342 2

Printing and binding at C&C Hong Kong.

Acknowledgements:

The publishers would like to thank the following
for their assistance with this book: the staff and
children at Herne Bay Junior School.

Picture acknowledgements:

Frank Lane Picture Agency/Minden Pictures 5 top;
Hodder Wayland Picture Library 1, 5 bottom, 6, 10,
12, 15, 16, 19 bottom, 20, 21 bottom (second from left
and far right), 23 bottom, 25 bottom, 26, 27; Robert
Pickett 4, 7, 9, 11, 13, 17 bottom, 18, 19 top, 21 top,
bottom (left and second right), 22, 23 top, 24, 25 top,
28, 29; WTPix 14, 17 top.

The photographs in this book are of models
who have granted their permission for their use
in this title.

Contents

What is personal hygiene?   4

Teeth   6

Tooth decay and gum disease   8

Oral hygiene   10

Skin   12

Exercise and sweating   14

What can go wrong with your skin?   16

Skin care   18

Hair   20

What can go wrong with your hair?   22

Hair care   24

Nails   26

Nail care   28

Glossary   30

Other books to read   31

Useful addresses   31

Index   32

What is personal hygiene?

Personal hygiene is all about keeping your body clean and healthy. Everybody wants to look good and stay healthy – and by following a few personal hygiene guidelines, you can keep your own body in tip-top condition.

◀ **Personal hygiene is important for everyone.**

Personal hygiene plays an important part in looking after your skin, hair, teeth and nails. Everybody looks different on the outside. Your skin might be pale or dark, and your hair might be long or short, straight or curly, brown or blonde. However, we are all much the same inside, and our bodies need to be looked after in the same ways.

!?/ Fantastic Facts

It's not just humans who need to keep their bodies clean! Some animals, like cats, wash by licking themselves, and many primates groom each other.

Nile crocodiles have an amazing arrangement. Tiny plover birds hop about inside their mouths. These birds pick off and eat the scraps of food that are left in between the crocodiles' teeth. The birds get a meal, and the crocodiles get their teeth cleaned!

▲ *This chimpanzee mother is grooming her baby to keep it nice and clean.*

Personal hygiene affects the way you look, and your health. If your skin is clean, your breath is fresh, your teeth are sparkly and your nails are clean and neat, you will look good. If you don't take care of yourself, though, you'll look grubby and unattractive and you can become unhealthy. It's up to you!

◄ *Looking after your body should make you look and feel good.*

Teeth

A newborn baby has no teeth. After about six months, the first teeth appear. By the time most toddlers are three years old, they have 20 milk or baby teeth. These start to fall out when the child is six or seven years old and are replaced by a full set of 32 permanent teeth.

▶ **This girl has lost her front milk teeth. Have you lost yours yet?**

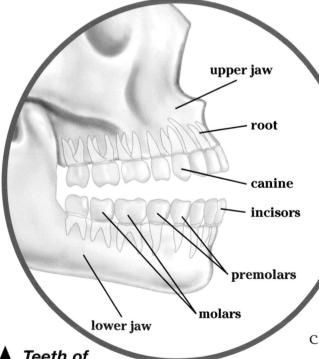

upper jaw

root

canine

incisors

premolars

molars

lower jaw

▲ **Teeth of different shapes do different jobs.**

Teeth are different shapes because they do different jobs. At the front of the mouth are sharp incisor teeth that are good for snipping. Pointed canine teeth next to the incisors are good for tearing. The premolars, which are behind the canines, have flatter surfaces for chewing. The biggest teeth are the molars at the back of the mouth. These allow us to chew and grind food so that it can be swallowed.

Each tooth has two main parts.

● The crown is the part you can see above the gum.

● The root is buried firmly into the jawbone inside the gum.

A tooth is made up of several layers. The outer coating is made of hard enamel. Underneath this is a softer layer called dentine. Right in the middle is the soft pulp that contains blood vessels and nerves.

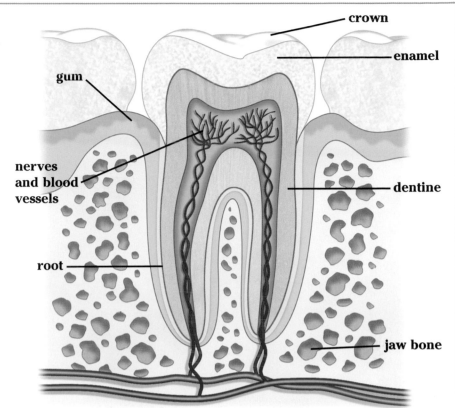

crown

enamel

gum

nerves and blood vessels

dentine

root

jaw bone

▲ *This picture shows the layers that make up a tooth.*

Action Zone

Find a mirror, open your mouth wide, and look closely at your teeth. Can you spot your incisors, canines, premolars and molars? How many of your teeth are milk teeth? How many are your permanent teeth?

▶ *When your milk teeth fall out they are replaced by permanent teeth.*

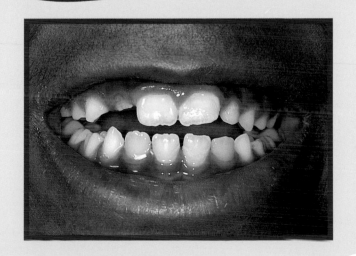

Tooth decay and gum disease

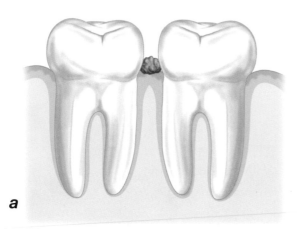

a

Tooth decay is caused by tiny organisms called bacteria. They are too small to be seen except with a microscope. They feed on any leftover sugar in your mouth.

Bacteria produce acid that eats into the teeth and makes holes in them. Unless the holes are filled by a dentist, they will just get bigger and bigger. Eventually you will end up with very bad toothache and the affected teeth may even need to be removed.

These diagrams show the process of tooth decay:
a) bacteria build up between the teeth
b) acid eats into the tooth
c) acid eats further into the tooth
d) the cavity reaches the nerve.

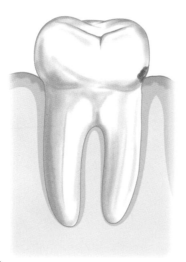

b

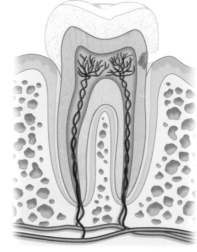

c

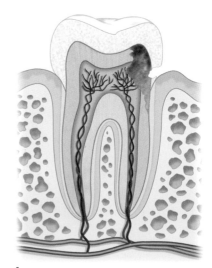

d

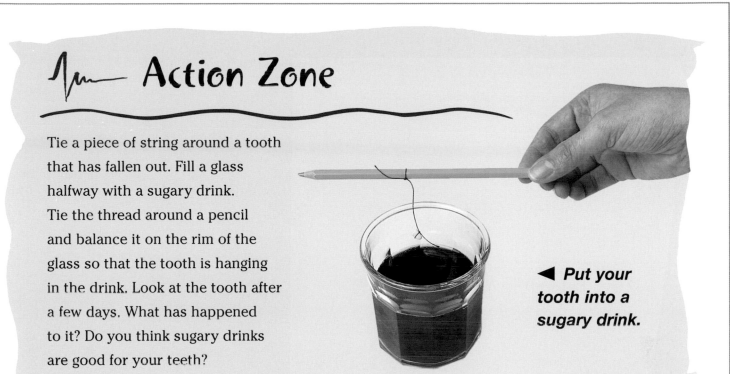

◄ **Put your tooth into a sugary drink.**

Bacteria can build up on and between the teeth. This forms a white material called plaque. If plaque is not removed, it becomes a hard material called tartar or calculus. This can spread down between the teeth and the gum, and make the gums red and sore. The gums may bleed, and the fibres that hold the tooth in place may become weakened. This means that the tooth may eventually become loose and fall out. Gum disease also makes your breath smelly and unpleasant.

▼ *By keeping your teeth nice and healthy you will always want to show them off when you smile.*

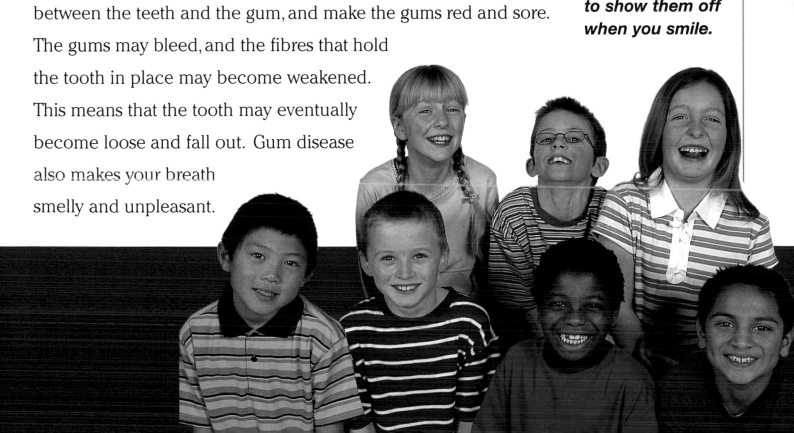

Oral hygiene

It makes sense to look after your teeth and gums. Follow these simple guidelines and you'll have a clean, healthy mouth:

● Brush your teeth at least twice a day. After breakfast and just before you go to bed are good times to do this. A small-headed toothbrush is easiest to use, with a pea-sized squirt of toothpaste. Many people like to use toothpaste that contains fluoride, because this gives extra protection against decay.

▲ *Brushing your teeth in the morning and evening helps to keep them in good condition.*

● Chewing a disclosing tablet before you brush your teeth can make your brushing more efficient. These tablets turn plaque a bright colour – often pink – so you can really see where the plaque is and can brush extra hard in those places.

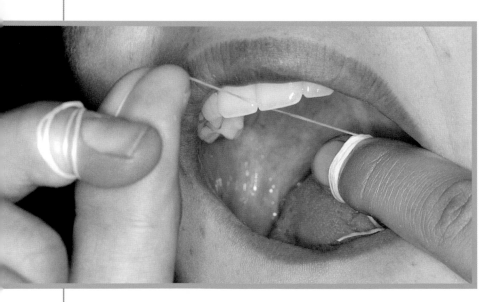

▲ *Using dental floss helps to clean your teeth where a toothbrush can't reach.*

● Using dental floss can help to remove any tiny scraps of food that are stuck between teeth.

• We all like sweets and fizzy drinks – but our teeth don't! Try to avoid eating sugary things between meals. Cheese, fruit, milk and bread are all tasty snacks and are much better for your teeth than chocolate and cola. Try to finish a meal with something non-sugary, so that sugar is not left around your teeth until the next meal.

• Rinsing your mouth with a mouthwash leaves a clean, fresh taste. It also makes your breath smell clean and fresh.

• Visiting a dentist regularly means that any problems are spotted before they become serious. Calculus can be removed before it damages your gums. Any cavities can be filled while they are still tiny.

• You can get advice about looking after your teeth and gums from your dentist. Other people can help you too – ask a school nurse if you have a problem.

▲ *A raw carrot is a tasty snack that is good for your teeth.*

▲ *There are many products to help you to look after your teeth and gums, including toothbrushes, dental floss, mouthwash and toothpaste.*

11

Skin

Your skin is your body's outer layer. It is a waterproof barrier that helps keep germs and dirt from getting into your body.

Your skin has three layers. Like every part of your body, skin is made up from millions and millions of tiny building blocks called cells. The outer layer of skin is made of flat, dead cells that are being worn away all the time. These are slowly replaced by the living cells below. The layer below this contains hair roots, nerve endings and tiny blood vessels.

▲ **Looking after your skin makes sure it stays clean and healthy.**

It also contains glands that produce oil and others that produce sweat. The innermost layer of skin contains fat for insulation and protection.

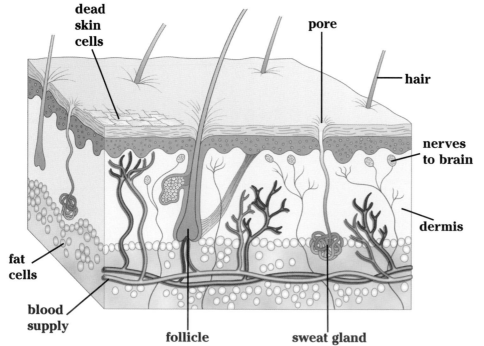

dead skin cells

pore

hair

nerves to brain

dermis

fat cells

blood supply

follicle

sweat gland

◀ **This diagram shows the different layers of skin.**

Although the skin all over your body has the same basic structure, there are some important differences. Skin is softer in some places than it is in others. It is also thicker in places. For example, eyelids have the thinnest skin. The soles of the feet and the palms of the hands have the thickest skin. The numbers of nerve endings, hairs, sweat glands and oil glands are also different in different places.

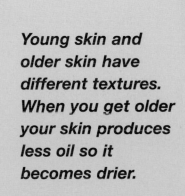

Young skin and older skin have different textures. When you get older your skin produces less oil so it becomes drier.

Exercise and sweating

Most people like doing some sort of sport or physical activity. You might enjoy gymnastics, cycling, dancing or judo. Being energetic is really good for your body, and helps to keep you fit and healthy.

▶ *Keeping active is great for your health.*

Whatever sport or activity you do, if you make your muscles work hard they will produce heat. Your skin plays an important role in making sure that your body does not get *too* hot. Sweat glands in your skin produce sweat, which trickles through tiny tubes to the surface. A tiny hole called a pore lets the sweat out of your skin. As it evaporates into the air it cools your body down.

▼ *Sweat from your sweat glands moves to the outside surface of your skin through tiny pores.*

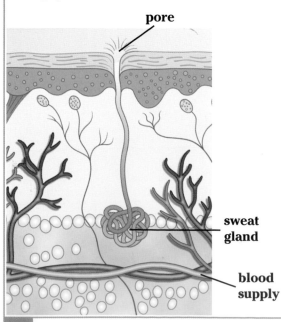

pore

sweat gland

blood supply

The skin under your arms contains more sweat glands than anywhere else in your body. Bacteria are attracted to the sweat they produce. The longer the sweat stays on the skin, the more bacteria can grow. If a lot of bacteria build up, they can start to produce an unpleasant smell.

Washing regularly helps to remove stale sweat. It also stops the bacteria building up and so you stay clean and fresh. There are usually showers in changing rooms so that you can freshen up after a sporting activity.

▼ *Having a bath or shower after physical activity is very important.*

 # Healthy Hints

Some people like to use anti-perspirants or deodorants. Deodorants contain chemicals that slow down the speed at which the bacteria build up. Anti-perspirants close some of the pores in the skin so that you produce less sweat. You can buy deodorants and anti-perspirants separately, but in many products they are combined. Some people like to use a roll-on, others choose a soft stick or an aerosol, while some people prefer not to use them at all – it's up to you!

What can go wrong with your skin?

Infections

Fungi are tiny organisms that can grow on the skin. They are too small to be seen without a microscope. Athlete's foot is a fungal infection that causes irritation and itchiness between the toes. Special creams and powders can usually completely cure the infection. You can avoid it by keeping your feet clean and making sure you always dry them thoroughly.

Viruses can infect the skin, causing warts. Often, a wart on the feet is called a verruca. If you have a verruca, you may be asked to wear a plastic sock or shoe at a swimming pool so that you do not pass the infection on to other people. There are several ways of treating verrucas and warts – and sometimes they just vanish on their own!

▼ *Keep your hands and feet clean to help to stop infections.*

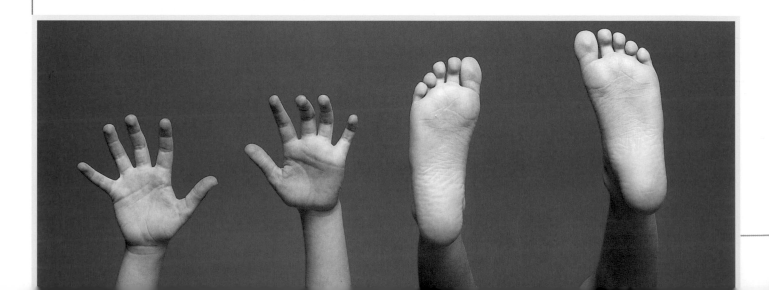

Sun damage

Skin can easily be damaged by strong light from the sun – and the fairer your skin is, the more easily it is damaged. A suntan may be attractive, but it is really bad for your skin. Too much strong sunlight can burn the skin, making it red and sore. Scientists have also shown that strong sunlight can lead to dry and wrinkled skin and to more serious conditions such as skin cancer.

▶ *Wearing hats and T-shirts protects you from the sun.*

🍎 Healthy Hints

These suggestions will help you to enjoy the sun safely:

- Wearing a sunhat protects your head and neck.

- Loose clothing such as a T-shirt is cool and protects your chest and back.

- Putting sunblock on your face, arms and legs – in fact, on any part of you that isn't covered up – will give you good protection.

- Sunlight is hottest, brightest and most dangerous around midday – so stay in the shade during that time.

▲ *Have fun in the summer sunshine – but remember to cover your skin.*

Skin care

It makes good sense to look after your skin so that it is clean and healthy. Here are some guidelines to help you:

● Your skin produces oil and other chemicals. Without washing, these soon build up so that you become grubby and smelly. Washing regularly helps to get rid of the oil and chemicals, as well as dirt and germs, which can cause spots, and dead skin cells. You may not be able to have a bath or shower every day, but do try to have a regular all-over wash. Remember to wash your face and neck every morning and night, and your hands more often.

► **Washing your face twice a day helps to keep your pores free from dirt.**

- Always wash your hands after using the toilet, to remove any germs. It is important to wash your hands before you eat, so that you do not transfer any germs on to your food.

- Remember to cover up in bright sunlight.

- Always use the footbath or shower at the swimming pool.

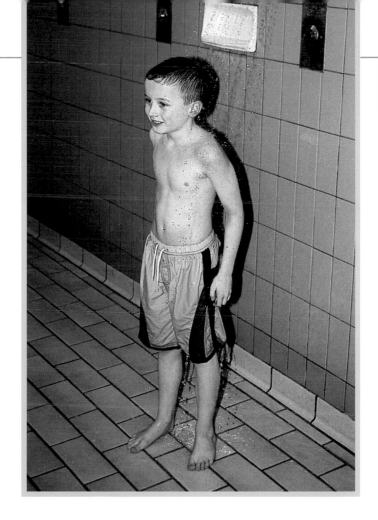

► *Using the footbath or shower before swimming can help to keep the pool clean for everybody.*

Action Zone

Most people use soap every day to wash with – but have you ever wondered what it is made of? Look at a bar of soap in its wrapper. Find the list of ingredients. Find some shower gel, or cleansing wipes – are any of the ingredients the same?

◄ *Washing your hands helps them to stay clean and fresh.*

Hair

Hair grows on our heads and on other parts of our bodies. Whatever its appearance, it has the same basic structure.

The part of each hair that you can see is called the shaft. The rest, the root, is buried in a tiny opening in the skin called a follicle. A hair is made of columns of dead cells. They contain a special protein called keratin which protects the hair. As new cells are made at the bottom of the root, the hair is pushed upwards, making it grow. The follicle eventually stops making new cells, so the hair becomes loose and falls out. A new one soon starts to grow in its place.

▲ *A healthy diet and lifestyle helps to keep your hair in good condition.*

The colour of your hair depends on how much pigment, called melanin, it contains. Dark hair contains a lot of melanin, while blond hair contains very little.

The texture of your hair depends on the shape of the hair follicles. Round follicles produce straight hair, oval follicles produce wavy hair and kidney-shaped follicles produce curly hair.

▼ *The shape of your hair follicles determines whether your hair is curly or straight.*

!?/ Fantastic Facts

Hair grows all the time, but not always at the same speed. It grows more quickly in warm weather than in cold, and more quickly at night than during the day! Some hairs last longer than others too. The hairs on your head may last several years, but eyelashes and eyebrows may last just a few weeks.

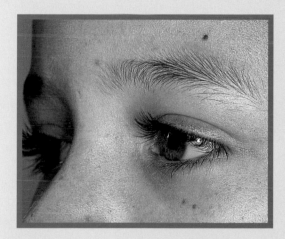

◄ *Your eyelashes and eyebrows often fall out, but they are always replaced by new ones.*

What can go wrong with your hair?

Many people have problems with their hair at some time – but most are not at all serious and can easily be dealt with.

Head lice

Head lice are tiny blood-sucking insects. Having head lice is not your fault and it does not mean that your hair is dirty. Head lice move easily from one person to another and are very common in schools. Lice can make the head feel itchy and sore.

▲ *This is a picture of a head louse. They are so small you need a microscope to see them in detail.*

Dandruff

Dandruff is just dead cells from the skin on the head. People with dry hair are more likely to have dandruff than people with oily hair. You can't 'catch' dandruff from other people.

Split ends

Individual hairs may split at the ends. You can avoid this by not using a very hot hairdryer. You can also have your hair trimmed regularly to remove the split ends.

◄ *Take care of your hair and it will look healthy and shiny.*

Damaging hair

Spending a lot of time in bright sunlight can damage your hair. Chemicals, such as the chlorine used to disinfect swimming pools, can also damage hair. Using tight elastic bands for ponytails and plaits can break the hair.

▶ **Protecting your hair with a swimming hat is a good idea.**

🍎 Healthy Hints

▲ **If you have head lice, ask an adult to help you get rid of them.**

If you have head lice, you will want to get rid of them quickly and easily. Some special shampoos and lotions are available that will kill the lice and the nits (the eggs laid by a female louse). You may prefer to use a very fine-toothed comb to remove the lice and nits. Your parents will know which is best for you; other people, such as your doctor, teacher and school nurse can also give you advice. The other members of your family should be treated too, just in case they also have lice.

Hair care

Clean, well-cared-for hair looks attractive. Here are some tips for looking after your hair:

● Washing your hair regularly helps to get rid of dirt, dead cells, oil and sweat. As you grow up, you may find that your hair gets greasy and you need to wash it more often. If you do need to wash it frequently, use a mild shampoo.

▲ *Washing your hair regularly keeps it looking good.*

● Drying hair can damage it unless you are careful. A gentle rub with a towel will take out a lot of water. Try not to drag a brush or comb roughly through knots and tangles – instead, use a comb with wide teeth and gently ease it through the tangle. If you use a hairdryer, set it on warm rather than hot.

◄ *Be careful not to pull at your hair if you brush it when it is wet.*

- Hair care products fill many shelves in supermarkets and chemists' shops. There are so many it's hard to choose. All you really need is a good shampoo and perhaps a conditioner occasionally.

- Hairdressers and barbers are important. Having your hair cut regularly keeps it looking good and gets rid of split ends.

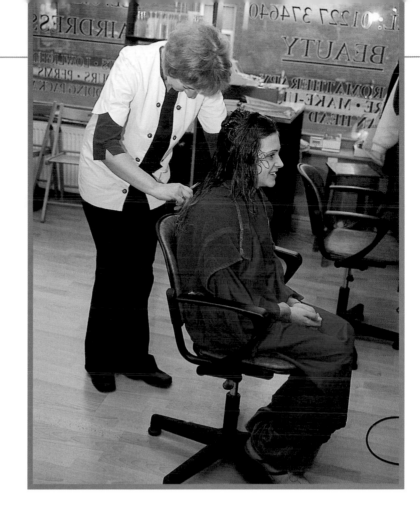

▶ *Having your hair cut keeps it in good condition.*

🍎 Healthy Hints

Just like the rest of your body, your hair needs the right building blocks to grow strong and look healthy. Try to eat plenty of fresh fruit and vegetables, and especially those that are rich in the vitamins and minerals that your hair needs. Carrots, green vegetables, fruits, liver and milk products are all good sources of Vitamin A. Vitamin A is particularly important for healthy hair – and skin too.

▶ *Fruit is a great source of vitamins.*

Nails

Nails, like hair, are made of dead cells that contain keratin. Each nail has a root under the skin. As new nail cells are made at the root, they push the other cells out and the nail grows. The thin covering around the base of the nail is called the cuticle.

Fingernails grow about 1 mm every week. They grow faster than toenails, and the longer the finger, the faster the nail grows!

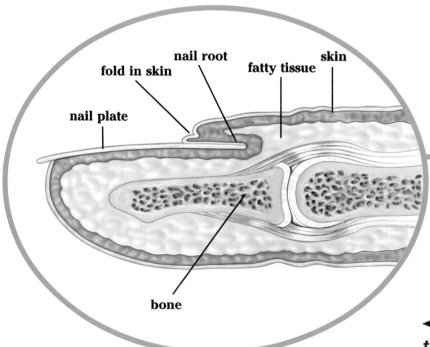

◄ Here you can see how the root of the nail lies hidden under the skin.

The material that nails are made of is thin and creamy white. Because the nail is semi-transparent, the blood vessels in the skin below it show through. This gives the nails a pink tinge. The half-moon at the base of the nail is thicker than the rest of the nail so the blood vessels cannot show through – and it looks white. The white spots that you sometimes see on your nails are usually slightly thickened areas that are caused when you bang the nail root.

▲ *Remember to clean under your nails with a scrubbing brush to remove any dirt.*

!?! Fantastic Facts

A man named Sridhar Chillal, from India, holds the record for growing the longest fingernails. He did not cut the nails on his left hand for more than 50 years, and they grew to more than one metre long! They were so heavy that they caused him a lot of pain and stopped him sleeping properly.

Nail care

Healthy nails can make your hands look clean and cared for – but if you don't take care of them it soon shows. Here are some tips:

● When you wash your hands, clean under your nails too. Dirt can build up quickly under nails.

● Keep your nails quite short. You can trim fingernails with scissors or nail clippers, or use an emery board to file them. Fingernails should have a rounded shape. Toenails need to be cut straight across with sharp scissors so that the edges do not grow into the toe itself.

▶ It is important to keep your nails short when playing sports such as netball.

● Nail polish can look very attractive – but not if it is neglected. Remove it as soon as it chips. Use nail polish remover to take one coat off before you apply a fresh coat.

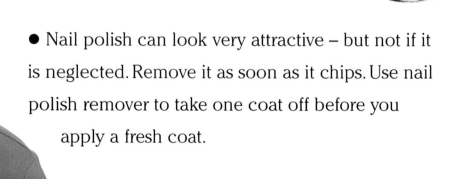

◀ Nail polish can look good if it is used properly. Don't use it all the time though as this is not good for your nails.

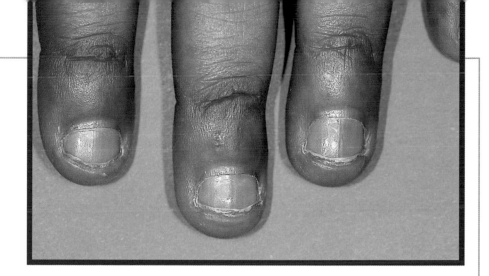

● Avoid biting your nails. It makes them weak, and can transfer germs and dirt into your mouth.

▶ *Bitten nails can look very ugly.*

 # Healthy Hints

Many people who bite their nails want to stop. There are several ways you can help yourself to do this. You can buy a special nail polish that tastes really horrible, so every time you get tempted to nibble a nail you get an unpleasant taste in your mouth! Give yourself a reward every day that you don't bite your nails. Cut out some pictures from magazines of some really gorgeous nails to remind yourself what you're aiming for. Good luck – you can do it if you really want to!

◀ *Try not to bite your fingernails like this girl.*

Glossary

acid a chemical that can wear away solids.

bacteria a micro-organism.

blood vessel one of a network of tubes that carry blood around your body.

calculus (also called tartar) hard material that builds up on teeth.

canine teeth sharp, pointed teeth at the sides of your mouth.

cavity a hole in a tooth.

cell one of the millions of tiny building blocks that make up your body.

dental to do with teeth.

dental floss thread used to clean between the teeth.

dentine the middle layer of a tooth.

disclosing tablet a tablet that, when chewed, colours plaque so you can see where you need to brush.

enamel the hard, outer coating of a tooth.

fluoride a mineral that helps to keep teeth strong.

follicle a tiny pit in the skin that contains a hair root.

fungus a type of micro-organism.

gland a part of the body that makes substances, for example, a sebaceous gland makes sebum (an oily substance).

hormone a chemical made by the body.

hygiene keeping clean.

incisor teeth the sharp, straight-edged teeth at the front of the mouth.

insulation to prevent loss of heat.

keratin a protein found in the skin, hair and nails.

melanin the chemical that gives skin and hair their colour.

micro-organism a living thing that is too small to be seen without a microscope.

minerals chemicals that our bodies need in tiny amounts to stay healthy.

molar teeth the large teeth at the back of the mouth.

nerves cells that carry messages to and from the brain.

oral to do with the mouth.

permanent teeth the second set of teeth.

pigment a chemical dye.

plaque material that builds up from bacteria on teeth.

pore a tiny hole.

premolar teeth the teeth between the canines and molars.

pulp the soft centre of a tooth.

verruca a type of wart that often appears on the feet.

virus a micro-organism that can cause illnesses.

vitamin a chemical that our bodies need to stay healthy.

wart a lump that grows on the skin.